AF488457

AN AIRPORT JOURNEY

Little feet, big adventures

Written by Emily Barrett

To all my past and future travel buddies: may you explore this great big world with curious eyes, kind hearts, and lots of love for all it has to offer.

✳ ✳ ✳

A big "thank you" to the families who trust me with their children, to the children who let me be their buddy in big and small adventures, and to the nannies and educators whose friendship and guidance help me along the way.

Little Luz is packing her suitcase, full of summery clothes, books, and MORE,

Including Stella the teddy bear, the one she mostly adores!

Tomorrow she will go on a trip to a place she hasn't been in a while.

Just thinking about it gives Little Luz the w i d e s t, brightest smile!

That **dark night**, Luz is *tossing* and *turning*, desperately trying to sleep,

her mind racing **full** of *joyful* thoughts, her excitement running deep.

She pictures the airport, where *speedy jets* and *gleaming planes* are soaring high.

Luz finally starts drifting off, dreaming about the **big blue** sky.

The morning after, Luz is bubbling with excitement, she can hardly wait.

Her energy bouncing as she skips over to mark today's date.

Her family chuckles, they are excited for this fun adventure too.

Before they are ready to leave, there are a few more things to do

Quickly using the bathroom, they hurry hurry HURRY to finish what's left to be done.

Leaving the house key with Mr. Arjun, who watches things while they are gone.

Mr. Arjun will water the plants and feed Vida, their old tabby friend,

Luz will miss her sweet cuddles, but knows she will be back in the end.

Off to the airport, with luggage in tow!

Traffic  crawls along slowly.

«ARE WE THERE YET? ARE WE THERE YET?»

Luz **really** wants to know.

The bus pulls up in front of the airport where Luz hops off, eager to fly.

Then she notices they must **wait** some more, and she lets out a soft cry.

Luz is feeling impatient, all she does is **waiting** for this trip to start.

Her frustration **builds**. She quickly clutches Stella closer to her heart.

Luz's body starts to calm down, her family now at the front of the line.

Their turn! She gives the agent her passport and points, "This bag is mine!"

Luz receives her printed boarding pass, now is it finally time **to go**?

She peeks *hopefully* at her family. They gently shake their heads "no".

Check - in
1
2
3

SECURITY

The next step is **SECURITY**, where agents check all you have packed with care,

To make sure everything's safe and sound for travelers everywhere.

Following the overhead signs, the family figures out where to go.

It feels crowded. Walking through the terminal is awfully slow.

The windy queues are never-ending, Luz wishes she could quickly zoom right past.

Her family lines up all their bags, Luz's coming the very last.

Next she walks through the big scanner and hears a loud beep that makes her feel scared.

Luckily, she remembers what to do right now - she came prepared!

Luz follows all directions and stretches her arms out with legs open wide.

A man with a serious face checks that she has nothing to hide.

Luz focuses on standing still as a statue, soon the process is done.

She picks up her little backpack and swiftly follows everyone.

20

They check out the departures monitor for the right number of their gate.

They must make their way over right now- they cannot risk being late!

Luz is starting to feel a bit nervous and wants Stella for a quick squeeze,

She digs down deep. She can't find the teddy bear! What now? Oh geez!

Luz then realizes she left Stella the bear in the security tray.

Panic kicks in, she can't just leave her special friend behind today!

She wants to turn around, run back to check for her teddy at lost and found,

but then her thoughts are interrupted by a loud announcement sound

Boarding is starting, she hears the loud call!

If she runs back now, she might miss it all.

A fellow traveler taps on her shoulder and holds out **Stella** the bear!!!

They point towards security and say "**You left your friend in there!**"

EXIT
GATE

Luz thanks the traveler and *hurries* to find her family at the gate.

They *line up* once more, feeling anxious but knowing it's **worth the wait.**

Luz shows her passport and boarding pass, which she holds out carefully and neat.

The gate agent has a peek and tells her where she can find her seat.

In the jet bridge it feels busy and hOt.

Luz squeezes through finding herself a good spot.

Excitement builds up as they move closer to the door.

Soon they'll be on the plane, finally ready to soar.

Luz remembers how to get to her seat and buckles herself tightly in,

Happily kicks off her shoes all set for the looooong flight to begin.

She takes out her sticker book, some new markers and sheets with word games too.

Luckily, she brought a backpack with fun activities to do.

Luz silently stares out the oval window as the rumbling plane takes off.

Everything looks tiny: the streets, the lush trees and pointy rooftops.

Luz starts to feel sleepy and getting comfortable is not working out.

She wiggles, she squirms, she stretches, she turns- feeling restless with a pout.

The flight turns **bumpy**, and a **sudden jolt** shakes Luz awake from her short nap.

She feels bothered being stuck with the seatbelt clipped across her lap.

Luz is fidgety and lets out a groan - she feels **really** bored!

She **can't** catch her family's attention and doesn't like being ignored.

Luz looks around and **really wants to shout,**

though she knows that's **not** the right way to let it out.

She takes a deep breath and gently squeezes her hand.

Wait! There is an announcement! It is time to land.

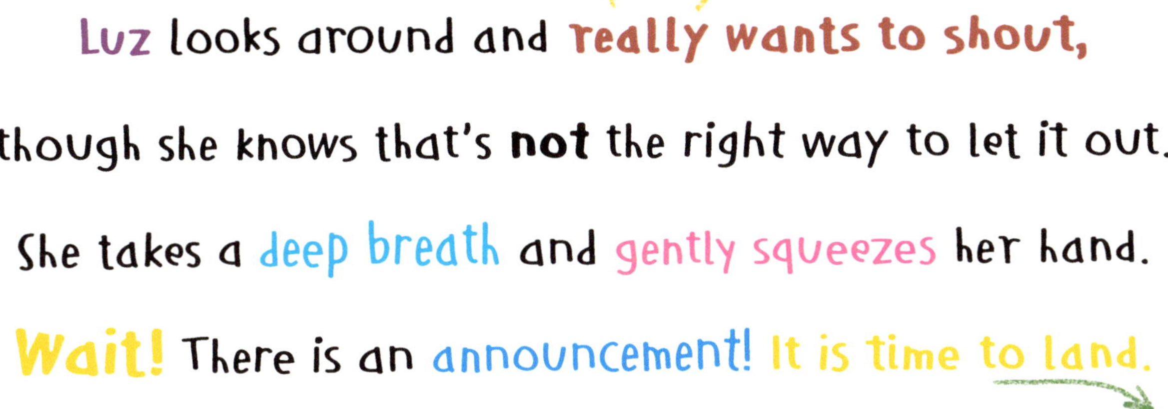

Luz starts to put away her books, disposes of her

trash and tidies her space.

She **can't wait** for the plane to land, joy shining

brightly on her face.

Luz feels her ears pop uncomfortably as the plane

gently goes lower,

She chews on her snack hoping for the discomfort

to be over.

31

Time to disembark the plane, Luz's row makes their way out through the entrance.

After the looooong journey, she is feeling a swirl of emotions at once.

Luz and her family need to pass by a desk that reads «**IMMIGRATION**».

The officer checks their papers and asks about their vacation.

IMMIGRATION

The line moves quickly, now through an underground walkway to find baggage claim.

Luz sees the luggage looping by on the belt, many look the same!

More passengers' suitcases are being added and keep going 

Finally, the five suitcases with their own nametags have been found!

With baggage piled on the trolley, Luz and her family walk out the door.

The air feels different! Luz twirls in a circle on the smooth floor.

She breathes a sigh of relief, after all this waiting it is time to roam,

On this exciting adventure far away from home.

Welcome Family

THE END.

Can you spot these objects hidden in the story?

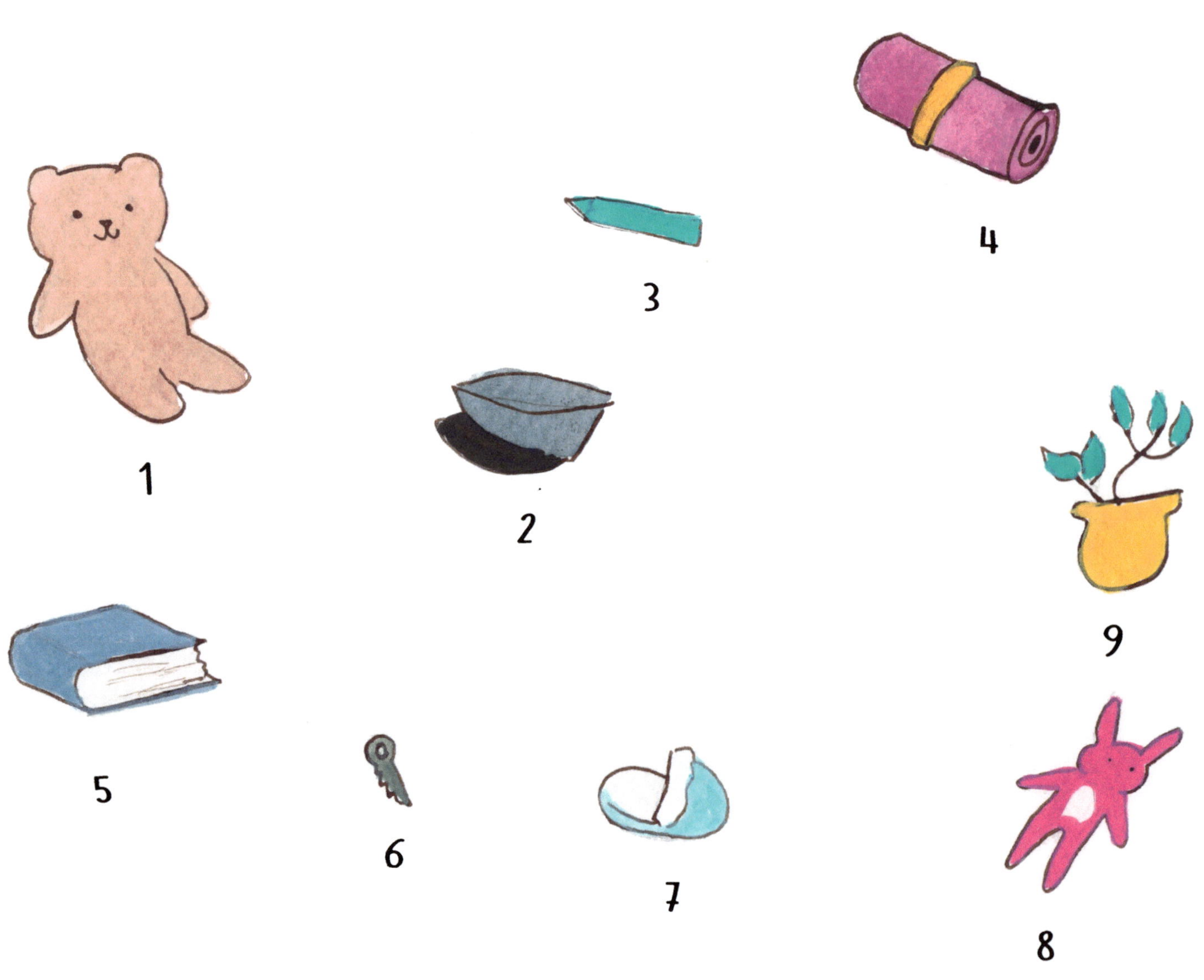

Flip back through the pages and see how many you can find!

9 798218 860080